The Duke of Milwaukee

The life and times of
Al Simmons
Baseball's Forgotten Superstar

By Ted Taylor

The Duke of Milwaukee

Prologue

Aloysius (or maybe it was Alois, depending on what researcher you quote) Harry Szymanski was born in Milwaukee, WI in May 22, 1902 as the fledgling American League was entering its second season.

The son of poor Russian/Polish immigrant parents, his father, the Pole, was a butcher. Al's mother was Russian. It was clear from early in his life that Al was destined to be a ball player, despite his father's wishes that he follow him in his line of work. Al was determined and his early boyhood coincided with the halcyon days of Connie Mack's Philadelphia Athletics and they became the young mid-westerner's favorite team.

Despite writing letters to Connie Mack as a teenager, suggesting that the A's send him train fare and offer him a contract, Mr. Mack seemed unaware of him until A's scout Ira Thomas discovered the young man playing for his hometown minor league team the Milwaukee Brewers.

Once with the A's Simmons and Mr. Mack developed a father-son relationship and when Al was inducted in to the Hall of Fame in 1953 he spent little of his acceptance speech on himself and most of it thanking Connie Mack. Priceless letters remain in Al's extended family reflecting the deep affection Mr. Mack had for his Hall of Fame protégé'.

Despite his prodigious numbers and awe-inspiring exploits on the diamond Simmons never really got his due in the news media of the day. Like another Philadelphia centerfielder, Richie Ashburn, Simmons played in the shadows of larger, superstars, like Jimmie Foxx on his own club and Babe Ruth and Lou Gehrig of the Yankees. Some would say that he was Gehrig to Jimmie Foxx's Ruth and that would be an accurate description. No pitcher of that day wanted to face either combination.

The Duke of Milwaukee

In researching this book I learned a lot of things about Al that I never suspected, among them was that he was a private man, more than a little stubborn, a bit cantankerous and seldom a very happy man. Writer Dale Smith described him as "intense, combative, temperamental, tenacious and self confident" and all seem to fit.

His grandson-in-law Patrick Greaber, an Atlanta GA businessman shared priceless anecdotes and family information about "The Duke" and his own father-in-law John Alan "Little Duke" Simmons – and the Little Duke's family, which included Greaber's wife Karen Ruth Simmons.

When respected baseball and Philadelphia A's historian, The Rev. Jerome Romanowski, suggested I write a book about Al Simmons – as a follow up to My *"Ultimate Philadelphia A's Research book"* I was surprised to learn that the only one ever done before was written in 1979 by Ed "Dutchie" Doyle and is long out of print. Hopefully this remedies that situation.

Ted Taylor

Table of Contents

Prologue	iii
Chapter 1 – How It All Began	1
Chapter 2 – Al Joins The Rebuilding A's	7
Chapter 3 – The Wonder Years, 1928-32	15
Chapter 4 – The White Sox Years, 1933-35	29
Chapter 5 – A Year as a Tiger, Two with the Nats	35
Chapter 6– Al shifts to the National League, chases 3,000 hits	39
Chapter 7– The 1940's..Al's Years as a Coach	43
Chapter 8– The Hall of Fame	49
Chapter 9– The Twilight Years	53
Chapter 10 – Al's Amazing Statistics	57
Chapter 11 – Al Simmons collectibles	65
Chapter 12 – The Greatest Team Ever	69
Selected Bibliography	73
Epilogue	77
About the Author	79
Index	81
And finally...	89

The Duke of Milwaukee

Photographs –
Philadelphia Athletics Historical Society
Ted Taylor Personal Collection
Al Simmons Family Archives – Patrick Greaber
Copyrights on others as indicated

© Ted Taylor, 2011
All Rights Reserved

To order additional copies of this book contact:
TTA Authentic LLC, P. O. Box 273, Abington, PA 19001

Published by
The Educational Publisher
www.EduPublisher.com
1313 Chesapeake Ave.
Columbus, OH 43212

ISBN: 1-934849-41-3
ISBN13: 978-1-934849-41-5

For my wife Cindy,
She always encourages me to do more!

Chapter 1 – How it all began

There's an oft-told story about a very young Aloysius Szymanski that suggests he came home one day from the fourth grade and announced to his father, a butcher, that he was going to become a professional baseball player. The elder Mr. Szymanski, a hard-working Polish immigrant, wasn't impressed and went on a rant about how his son would not do anything so foolish and to illustrate his concern the old man administered a whipping with a leather strap. The family was poor, times were tough, and Al's father wanted nothing to do with his son playing the game of baseball for a living.

"Now what do you want to do with your life?" the older man said after the whipping, and a defiant boy said, "I still intend to become a baseball player". Seeing that his influence wasn't going to produce another butcher in the family his father said, "By God you'd better be a good one". And Al did.

Al's father passed away while Al was still young, but he supported his beloved mother for the rest of her life.

According to family lore, after high school Al went to college, such as it was, as a football player. This was 1920. The school, now the University of Wisconsin – Stevens Point, was then Stevens Point Normal School, a two-year institution for budding teachers. Al didn't graduate, in fact he likely didn't stay long after the end of the football season.

An inquiry to the school turned up no record of him at all. Laura Gehrman Rottier, Director of Alumni Affairs said, "I looked through our database, consulted with Registration and Records on multiple spellings, talked with Athletics and looked through our 1920 and 1921 yearbooks. At this point, we have no record of anyone named Aloysius Syzmanksi or Szymanski or Al Simmons. It is certainly possible he attended here we cannot confirm that with any documentation."

Maybe he went to college, maybe he didn't. It wasn't unusual in those days for athletes to "shop" their talents to institutions of higher learning and really never attend to the mundane things, like showing up for class.

The Duke of Milwaukee

Al's Grandson-in-law Patrick Greaber (married to Al's son's daughter Karen Ruth Simmons) said, "I'm sure that he went to college to play football, but I'm also sure he really wasn't all that interested in getting an education. He saw his future in sports."

It was also about this time in his life that the very athletic young man also considered becoming a heavyweight fighter. He decided, however, that hitting a baseball could be a more lucrative pastime than punching someone's lights out – or getting yours punched out in return. Greaber said that Al loved boxing and had many friends among members of the sweet science. "We know that Al boxed as an amateur and we have a couple of trophies that he won."

We do know that in 1920 when spring rolled around Al joined the Juneau Millers, a semi-pro club located in the county seat of Dodge County, Wisconsin – about an hour's drive from Milwaukee. He was, after all, a baseball player.

It was probably in 1921 that young Mr. Szymanski actually wrote a letter to Connie Mack offering to come to Philadelphia for the price of a train ticket.

Connie Mack

The Duke of Milwaukee

In his 1950 book "*My 66 Years in the Big Leagues*" Connie Mack writes, "Do you remember the great Al Simmons? He wrote to me in 1921 that he was looking for a job and would come to Philadelphia if I would pay his train fare. That's when I missed the train. I didn't send him the car fare and Al signed with Milwaukee. As a result I had to buy him after he had made good."

Prior to becoming the A's manager – with the formation of the American League in 1901 – Mr. Mack had been skipper of the minor league Milwaukee Brewers for four years.

Al was signed by Otto Borchert, owner of his hometown Milwaukee club in 1921. Borchert promptly sent the strapping 19-year-older (6-foot, 200-pounder) to Aberdeen, SD, of the Class D Dakota League to begin the next season. In 99 games there the big outfielder hit .365 and was recalled by the American Association Brewers for the last 19 games of the season – where he batted just .220, 11-hits in 50 at-bats.

The next season, 1922, found him at Shreveport of the Texas League where the pitchers were no match for him and he batted .360 (with 12 homers) in 144 games. The Brewers, again, recalled him and in 24 contests with them he hit .398 (39-for-98).

Feeling snubbed by the A's and still under contract to Milwaukee, Simmons decided that, maybe, he could play for John J. McGraw's New York Giants. He wrote a letter to Roger Bresnahan, who was skipper of the Giants' American Association Toledo club and said he'd come to the Giants for $150 and expenses. Hall of Famer Bresnahan never got back to him. Simmons was now 0-for-2 in direct contacts to big league clubs.

In later years Simmons said that he was glad that the Giants never followed up his letter because "I'm not so sure I'd have enjoyed playing for McGraw. Both of us were hot heads and we would have surely clashed". The irony, of course, is that Connie Mack and John J. McGraw never liked each other – not for a minute - and had McGraw known that Mack was about to trade for Simmons he'd have likely signed him out of spite.

But at the urging of his close friend and chief scout Ira Thomas, on December 15, 1923 Connie Mack gave himself and Philadelphia baseball fans an early Christmas present. Instead

The Duke of Milwaukee

of train fare it cost Mr. Mack $50,000 and three players to get Simmons from the Brewers.

Al had, by then, changed his name to Simmons because the newspapers constantly butchered the spelling of Szymanski. As legend has it, one day Al looked at a billboard at the Milwaukee ball park and there was an advertisement for "Simmons Hardware" on it. On that day his name changed.

The actual transaction sent outfielder Wid Matthews, outfielder Frank "Beauty" McGowan and infielder Heinie Scheer from the A's to the American Association club. Many, this author included, believe it was the best trade that Connie Mack ever made. Matthews played in just 192 games over three big league seasons (.284 batting average), McGowan played in 375 games over five seasons (.262 lifetime) and Scheer never got back to the big leagues after 120 games in two A's campaigns and a .212 batting average.

The Duke of Milwaukee

The Duke of Milwaukee

Chapter 2 – Al Joins the Rebuilding A's

The Philadelphia Athletics were nothing short of dreadful from 1915 through the dawn of the 1920's. After suffering through seven lean years, and establishing a record for gross ineptitude, Mr. Mack decided it was time to re-build his baseball fortunes.

When World War I ended and players were, again, available Connie, always a keen judge of talent, kept his eyes on prospective players in the minors, on the campus and on the sandlots. One year the A's mentor tried out over 300 players at Shibe Park. Giving try-outs to semi pro players was something he did all his life. Mr. Mack was never a fan of owning his own farm clubs.

Some say things actually began to change over Labor Day weekend of 1918 when A's scout Tom Turner brought in nine rookies – including Jimmy Dykes, Chick Galloway, Red Wingo and Glenn Myatt. And while they didn't stimulate an immediate change in the A's fortunes they did form the early building blocks of what was to come.

Jacob Ruppert, the owner of the New York Yankees once commented, "Mack must have the Philadelphia fans hypnotized, any other manager would have been run out of town." Mack, of course, was not a hypnotist, but he did own 50 per cent of the ball club.

In 1922 the A's added bleachers in left field at Shibe Park and the Philadelphia club led the league in homers with 111. Tilly Walker had 37 of them. Eddie Rommel went 27-13 for the Mackmen and they emerged from the cellar. The 1923 A's amazed everyone by battling the Yankees for the AL lead well in to June.

"The Roaring 20s", Mack decided was a good time to be a winner. In his book Mack wrote, "The time had come to rebuild our team. This meant, as it does in any business, heavy investments." Mack went out and purchased Sammy Hale for $75,000 and Paul Strand for $40,000 (purchased the same day Mr. Mack signed Simmons). He also brought in Joe Hauser from

The Duke of Milwaukee

Milwaukee, acquired Bing Miller from Washington, bought Maxie Bishop from Jack Dunn's Baltimore Orioles, Freddie Heimach from Camden and Rube Walberg from the Northwest.

Strand, who had earlier failed with the Boston Braves, looked terrific at Salt Lake City in 1923 batting .394 with 43 homeruns. No one factored in the rarified air of the Salt Lake and Strand laid an egg with the '24 A's appearing in just 47 games and batting .228. The A's released him and he never got another shot in the majors.

Hale, while not a revelation, did stick with the A's for seven seasons and saw service as, mostly, a third baseman. But the investment of $115,000 for these two players showed that Mack was serious.

Actually his best deal of that time was when he traded three marginal players – and added $50,000 to the deal – for Al Simmons.

In spring training 1924 the sportswriters were all over Mack. "This kid can't hit" some wrote, "he stands with his foot in the bucket".

Indeed he did.

The experts noticed that when Al took his stride to swing at the ball he pulled his left foot back (one writer said, "like a timid kid fearful of the pitcher") but it didn't matter, he tore the cover off the ball and earned his lifelong moniker "Bucket Foot Al" (which he hated).

Harry Robert, a sports reporter, approached Mack in spring training and asked him if he intended to change Simmons' batting style. The Tall Tactician looking at the young reporter as if he was an idiot replied, "Young man, anyone who hits the ball like that can stand on his head at the plate if he wants to."

Manager Connie Mack recognized his natural batting talent and would not allow anyone to change his style. Mack turned out to be right about the untested rookie. Simmons batted .308 in his first year and raised his average to .384 in his second. In only his second year on the team, Simmons led the A's in every hitting category. Simmons also became the first player in American League history to knock in 100 or more runs in his first two seasons in the majors. Simmons was also an excellent outfielder.

The Duke of Milwaukee

Now on a roll, Mack continued to build his ball club and he added outfielder Bill Lamar from Toledo, playboy slugger Rollie Naylor and then forked over $100,600 to Jack Dunn for Lefty Grove and another $50,000 to Portland for catcher Mickey Cochrane.

Some felt the A's might win the AL pennant in 1925 and they could have, some believe, except they lost slugging first baseman Joe Hauser (who had 27 homers in 1924) in spring training when he cracked his knee cap fielding a routine grounder. His replacement that season was Jim Poole, who Mack acquired from Portland. Poole batted .294 in 101 games at the initial sack. Joe was never the same again and, when he returned in 1926, he batted just .192.

Hauser, like Simmons, was a Milwaukee native – and three years older than Al. He twice hit 60-plus homeruns in the minors, bashing 63 for Baltimore in 1930 and an incredible 69 for Minneapolis in 1933. He was truly "The Homerun King of the Minors".

Simmons batted .343 for the third place A's in 1926. He played in 147 games and stroked 19 homeruns and drove in 109. Lefty Grove was just 13-13, the most wins on the staff, but things were taking shape.

The injury to Hauser, of course, eventually opened the door for what Mr. Mack once called his "greatest gift" when his former star Frank "Homerun" Baker, now a scout, delivered a young farm boy – six years Al's junior - from Sudlersville, MD named James Emory Foxx.

In 1927 Mr. Mack was going all out and looking for gate attractions. He signed the 40-year-old Ty Cobb and 39-year-old Zack Wheat, both future Hall of Famers. When they joined the A's it is the stuff of legends that Simmons, the centerfielder, reportedly went to Mr. Mack and said that if he had to play center between "those two old men, I'll be worn out by June". Actually Al only saw action in 105 games that year and batted .392 (best in the league, but not enough at-bats to qualify for the batting title).

The Duke of Milwaukee

**Eddie Collins, Ty Cobb, Tris Speaker
A's Hall of Fame "bench" 1928**

Mr. Mack also brought back Eddie Collins, age 40, as a player and sometimes coach (he got in to 95 games, hit .338), and Kid Gleason as a coach.

Mack also tried for Tris Speaker in 1927 but the "Gray Eagle" signed with Washington instead, though he did come on board with the A's in 1928.

Actually the Athletics' addition of Ty Cobb helped Simmons become an even better hitter. The two easily became friends, which may have added to Simmons's growing infamy. As his fame grew, so did his reputation of his temper and hatred for pitchers. He was quoted saying, "I hate all pitchers. They are trying to take the bread and butter out of my mouth." Opposing hitters also disliked him more and more as well. Simmons became quite an agitator all the way from his position in left field.

Cobb and Simmons both got ejected – and suspended – for an incident in a May 5 game with the Red Sox. Cobb had hit a ball over the right field fence in the eighth inning with the A's trailing 3-2. Everyone could see that the ball was fair when it went over and then curved foul. Umpire Red Ormsby ruled the ball foul, though virtually everyone in the park but him knew it was fair when it left the yard. During his next at-bat Cobb swung his bat, missed the ball, but hit Ormsby in the chest. All heck broke loose. Cobb said it was an accident, Ormsby said it was

The Duke of Milwaukee

deliberate. Simmons flew from the dugout to defend his new friend and pushed and jostled Ormsby in the argument. Ormsby ejected both men and debris rained from the grandstands.

AL President Ban Johnson suspended both players and Mr. Mack was not pleased. Long an ally of Johnson, this turned Mack against him and, ultimately, he cast the deciding vote that ended Johnson's 27-year-reign as the league's chief executive.

Cobb had a positive influence on Simmons and sportswriters of the day commented that "the Milwaukeean flashes many of the mannerisms of Ty Cobb. Some of this is natural while part is copied due to their close association on the A's". The fact was that Al, like, Cobb didn't like the press and both of them were notoriously difficult interviews. Al was, according to Greaber, a very private man and this would account for the fact that in researching this book actual news media quotes from Al were quite scarce.

Despite his reputation on the field, Simmons was getting almost as much fan mail as Babe Ruth – who became a good friend of Al's over the years. It should be noted however, that he received most of his letters from female admirers and not star-stuck boys. With his good looks and flashy clothes, Simmons loved the nightlife and a good cigar.

Connie Mack and his star outfielder, Al Simmons

The Duke of Milwaukee

In 1928 it was the Yankees and the A's – and then the rest of the American League. It was nip and tuck all season, but when the A's won the Yankees won and when the A's lost so did the Yankees. The Yankees had a 13-game lead on July 4 but by September 7 the A's, who had trampled the opposition in the second half of the season, had a half-game lead. They accomplished this by sweeping back-to-back doubleheaders against the Red Sox.

The Mackmen headed to Yankee Stadium for a season-ending series with the Bronx Bombers. And with more than 82,000 people in the stadium the A's lost 5-0 to George Pipgras. The A's then dropped the second game 7-3 and then split the remaining two games of the series. They went from being in first place to being a game-and-a-half out.

The late Tommy Henrich of the Yankees recalled a story told him by Hall of Famer Bill Dickey. When the A's came to town for his crucial series the Yankees held a meeting as to what to do about the A's big hitters – Foxx, Cochrane, Haas and Simmons. Dickey recalled that someone suggested that it would be a good idea to rough Simmons up, to knock him down a little bit. "So we roughed him up," Dickey said, "In the four game series, he had eleven hits, ten of them for extra bases." Henrich said that Simmons "hated the Yankees", but added, "I liked him, I liked the way he would bear down on us."

For the second straight season Al missed a considerable number of games (40) and those missed contests ultimately would cost him his shot at 3,000 hits. For the year he batted .351 with 15 homers and 107 RBI's.

Years later Ty Cobb told reporters that had he not quit the ball club in early September he felt that he might have been the ingredient needed to dethrone the New Yorkers. Cobb, age 41, was batting .323 when he retired. Actually Cobb had wanted to retire before the 1928 season but Connie Mack talked him out of it, suggesting that it would be an experience for Cobb to play in the same outfield with Tris Speaker. In a Universal wire service story dated March 5, 1928 Cobb said, "Tris is a great player and if we both play together we will give them something to think about. But we'll let that rest with Connie Mack."

The Duke of Milwaukee

The Yankees held on to win the pennant in 1928 but it was their last trip to the big dance for awhile. The era of Connie Mack's last juggernaut was about to begin.

© Bruce F. Murray
Al and comedian Joe E. Brown at the '29 World Series

The Duke of Milwaukee

Chapter 3 – The Wonder Years, 1929-32

They called Al a warrior. He disliked pitchers (much like another Philadelphia Hall of Famer, Rich Ashburn, who said they were trying to take the food out of the mouths of his children), he was intent on damaging the enemy, demolishing pitchers with his bat, stifling rallies with his glove and upsetting infielders with vicious take-out slide (he was Pete Rose, before there was a Pete Rose).

Despite playing nothing but day games, he never seemed to tan. Perhaps it was his Polish genes. In fact his most evident characteristic was his pale complexion. His face would grow whiter as he concentrated on a tense situation.

McNair, Grove, Bishop, Haas, Boley, Walberg, Schang, Lew Krause, Moore, Summa, Williams, Earnshaw.
Mahaffey, Quinn, Rommel, Higgins, Perkins, Cochrane, Dykes, Connie Mack, Simmons, Miller, Foxx.
Collins, Gleason.

The 1929 Athletics – the best team of All-time

In 1929 Al was named the American League's "Most Valuable Player" by *The Sporting News,* baseball's Bible. He batted .365 (second in the AL), clouted 34 homers (trailing only Ruth's 46, and Gehrig's 35) and led the AL with 157 RBI's, three more than Babe Ruth. He led the league in total bases with 373, was third in hits with 212 and was second to Ruth in slugging average with .642. He also tied Frank Schulte for best fielding average with .989.

In August 1996 *Sports Illustrated* came out with an issue "The Team That Time Forgot" with Al Simmons on the cover. It spoke of the remarkable 1929 A's who many believe was the greatest baseball team ever assembled.

William Nack wrote, "From 1929 to 1931, the Philadelphia A's were the best team in baseball, with four future Hall of Famers in the lineup (Foxx, Simmons, Cochrane, Grove) that dominated Babe Ruth's legendary Yankees. So why hasn't anyone heard of them?"

His article, ironically, came a year after this writer and Ernie Montella formed the Philadelphia Athletics Historical Society. We were devoted to making sure that the A's were not forgotten and that people who might have forgotten how good they really were would take the time to remember. And boy were those teams good.

A's 1929 Murderer's Row – Cochrane, Simmons, Haas, Foxx and Miller

The A's had a great year in 1929 winning 104, losing 46 and finishing an amazing 18 games ahead of the second place

Yankees. Jimmie Foxx at first base batted .354 with 33 homers and 117 RBI's (he was just 21), Max Bishop was on second, Joe Boley played short, Sammy Hale and Jimmy Dykes split third. In the outfield Al Simmons batted .365 with 34 homers and a league-leading 157 RBI's, joined by Mule Haas (.313, 16 homers, 82 RBI's) and Bing Miller (.335, 8 homers, 93 RBI's). Mickey Cochrane caught 135 games, batted .331 and drove in 95 runs). On the mound the staff was led by George "Moose" Earnshaw with a 24-8 mark, Lefty Grove 20-6 and Rube Walberg 18-11. Coach Eddie Collins, now 42, even got in to nine games and served as a link with Mr. Mack's earlier championship clubs.

Actual scored page from '29 World Series program, note that Al Simmons and KiKi Cuyler were reporting for the Chicago Daily News

But what made this team even more special was the way they handled the Chicago Cubs in the World Series.

Under Joe McCarthy the Baby Bruins would win the National League crown by 10-and-a-half games over the Pittsburgh Pirates. The Cubs were loaded with talent with players like Rogers Hornsby (.380), KiKi Cuyler (.360) and the slugging Hack Wilson (.345, 39 homers, 159 RBI's). On the mound they had Pat Malone (22-10), Charley Root (19-6) and Guy Bush (18-7) as their top three hurlers.

The Duke of Milwaukee

The A's took game one in Chicago 3-1 when Mr. Mack fooled everyone and started 35-year-old Howard Ehmke in game one instead of Earnshaw or Grove. Most people thought Mack had lost his mind, but in the end he had the last laugh. Ehmke hurled a complete game and gave up the only run of the day the Cubs would score in the ninth inning. To be fair, Root, who was relieved by Bush in the eighth inning also pitched well enough to win.

Game two saw Earnshaw start against Malone. Earnshaw lasted until the fifth inning when Grove came in to relieve him. The A's won 9-3.

Back to Philadelphia for game three, the Cubs badly needed a win and they got one, 3-1, with Bush beating Earnshaw who had started back-to-back games.

For game four, Mack went the geriatric route again and started 45-year-old Jack Quinn. The Cubs countered with Root. This was a game that has become legendary.

Quinn did not possess Ehmke's magic and left the game after six innings trailing 7-0. Rube Walberg came in and the Cubs added another run in the seventh.

Trailing 8-0 the A's were being mocked unmercifully from the Cubs dugout. Guy Bush put a blanket over his head and did an Indian war dance in the dugout. But things were about to change.

Simmons came to the plate and smashed Root's third pitch on to the top of the left field pavilion at Shibe Park. It was 8-1.

Jimmie Foxx, first of 4 straight singles

18

The Duke of Milwaukee

The homerun was followed by four straight singles (Foxx, Miller, Dykes and Boley). It was 8-3.

Pinch-hitter George Burns made the first A's out of the seventh batting for pitcher Rube Walberg. Bishop then singled to center and Dykes scored. It was 8-4.

Manager McCarthy yanked Root and brought in reliever Art Nehf. In typical Philly fashion, Root left the field to a chorus of boo's.

Mule Haas was the first one to face the new hurler and he hit a low liner to center where outfielder Hack Wilson lost the ball in the sun. Boley and Bishop both scored and Haas raced around the bases for an inside-the-park homerun. It was now 8-7 and no one was doing any dances in the Cubbies dugout.

Jimmy Dykes was so excited in the A's dugout that he pounded the man standing next to him on the back. The man was the manager, Connie Mack, who fell in to the bat rack and spilled many of them. "I'm sorry," Dykes said and Mr. Mack, picking himself up off the floor said, "that's all right Jimmy, wasn't it wonderful?"

Cochrane was the next batter and Nehf walked him. McCarthy brought in Sheriff Blake from the bullpen – but it wouldn't have mattered if he brought the entire Chicago police force at this point.

Simmons greeted the Sheriff with a single to left, Foxx then singled up the middle scoring Cochrane and the game was tied at 8-8.

Again McCarthy went to his bullpen, this time he trotted in their ace, Malone, who was to face Bing Miller. Instead of getting Miller out, he hit him with a pitch and the bases were loaded.

The next batter was Dykes who hammered a pitch in to deep left where Riggs Stephenson briefly had it – and dropped it – allowing two more runs to score. The A's were up 10-8.

As an anti-climax Malone struck out both Joe Boley and Burns, batting for the second time in the inning as a pinch-hitter, to end the frame.

Mack trotted out Lefty Grove for the final two innings and it was almost unfair. The big 6'3 lefty, some say the hardest thrower in baseball ever, retired the Cubs and the A's had a 3-1 lead in the series.

The Duke of Milwaukee

Simmons scores the go-ahead run in the 7th

The A's ended it the next day in Philadelphia coming back with three runs in the ninth inning to beat the Cubs 3-2. Walberg, who relieved Emhke in the fourth, got the win, Malone took the loss.

Up to that ninth inning Malone had allowed just two hits – one each to Simmons and Miller. The Cubs were three outs away from taking the series back to the friendly confines of Wrigley Field.

Walter French struck out to start the ninth for the Mackmen. Max Bishop was next and he slashed a single up the third base line. Mule Haas was up next and blasted one of Malone's offerings over the make-shift rooftop bleachers on North 20th Street. It was 2-2. The Shibe Park faithful came to life, reports of the day said the place was in an uproar. The fans could sense the 'kill" and President Herbert Hoover, who was in attendance that day and was getting ready to depart, sat back down.

Mickey Cochrane batted next and Malone got him to ground out to Hornsby at second. But Malone's worries were not over. The next batter up, with the game on the line, was Al Simmons.

Armed with his 38-inch long bat the burly Milwaukee mauler stepped to the plate and hit a drive to right center that looked like it had a chance to get out of the park, but fell in and Al would up with a double. Jimmie Foxx was next and Malone walked him intentionally, setting up a force at three bases. The under appreciated Bing Miller was next. Malone buzzed two fastballs by the outfielder for strikes and then, on the next pitch, Miller choked up and plopped one over Hornsby's head in to right field with Simmons charging home with the winning run.

Fifteen days after the A's won their first World's Series since 1913 – October 29, 1929 – came "Black Tuesday" and the start of a depression that would, eventually, put Mr. Mack and his A's on the brink of financial collapse for years to come and would necessitate the dismantling of his last great teams.

Al was always a gamer and one story is told about how he burst a blood vessel in his knee in the 15th inning of the first game of a doubleheader on Memorial Day 1930 against Washington. The team doctor didn't want to leave the ball park and miss the second game so he advised Mr. Mack that it would be okay to keep Al on the bench in the event they needed him as a pinch hitter. Eventually, with the A's losing 7-5 in the nightcap Mr. Mack sent Simmons to the plate as a pinch hitter. The bases were loaded in the bottom of the ninth and Al, who was in serious pain and clearly limped to the plate, avoided having to run hard by delivering a grand slam homerun and an 9-7 victory.

Washington owner Clark Griffith said after that game, "Simmons hit 14 of his 34 homers in the eighth or ninth inning and every one figured importantly in the final score. We were never the same after he licked us in that doubleheader."

Hall of Famer Charlie Gehringer once told author Donald Honig, "Simmons hit the most wicked ground balls to second base. Simmons was pitched outside to negate his pull-hitting power and he'd hit to the right side and slice them, he could really blister it."

The Duke of Milwaukee

Lefty Grove, 28-game-winner in 1930

The A's won the pennant again in 1930 finishing eight games ahead of Walter Johnson's second place Washington Senators. Lefty Grove won 28 games (against just 5 losses), Earnshaw finished 22-13 and Walberg won 13 (against 12 losses). Foxx hit 37 homers and batted .335, Simmons hit 36 homers and batted a league-leading .381, Cochrane batted .357, Miller hit .303 and Haas chipped in at .299. Jimmy Dykes, now the regular third sacker, batted .301.

Gabby Street's St. Louis Cardinals won the NL crown finishing two games ahead of the Cubs. The Cardinals didn't have the star power of the A's, but did feature Frankie Frisch, Charley Gelbert, Chick Hafey and Jimmy Wilson. Their top pitcher was Wild Bill Hallahan who went 15-9 for the season.

The A's started Lefty Grove in game 1 of the World Series and came home a 5-2 winner. The A's went up 2-games-to-none with a 6-1 win at Shibe Park. Earnshaw got the win, Flint Rehm the loss.

Home was sweet for the Cardinals and they won game three at Sportsman's Park 5-0 with Hallahan pitching a complete game. Earnshaw took the loss for the Mackmen.

The Cards evened the series at two each with a 3-1 win in game four. Jesse Haines got the win, Grove the loss. Both men pitched complete games.

Earnshaw and Grove (in the eighth inning) combined to toss a three-hit shutout in game five and the A's came away with a 2-0 win. Burleigh Grimes took the loss for St. Louis.

The A's then made it two World's Championships in-a-row drubbing the Cards 7-1 at Shibe Park. Earnshaw pitched a complete game five-hitter while the Cards used four pitchers and Hallahan took the loss.

In the spring of 1931 Al, already one of the games' highest paid players signed a three year contract with the A's for $100,000 ($33,333.33-per-year). The White Sox ended up paying the last of the contract (1933) and probably were responsible for the penny it took to make it an even $100k. That salary made Simmons the second highest player in the majors, trailing only the $80,000 annually paid to Babe Ruth.

The year 1931 would bring the A's their third straight AL flag. Connie Mack's A's finished 13-and-a-half games ahead of Joe McCarthy's New York Yankees.

A's hurler Lefty Grove recalled Al in Donald Honig's *Baseball When the Grass was Real.* "The league was chock full of hitters in those days. You had guys like Goose Goslin, George Sisler, Baby Doll Jacobson, Ty Cobb, Tris Speaker, Harry Heilmann, Joe Sewell, Babe Ruth, Lou Gehrig. Gee whiz. In those days if you didn't hit .300 they didn't think much of you.

"With us, Al Simmons, Jimmie Foxx and those guys. Simmons was great. Bucket foot Al. Always pulled that left foot down the third base line when he swung at the ball. Like to spike the third baseman. Big long bat, long as the law allowed. Could he ever hit that ball. Whew! One year he held out until the season started – finally signing for $100,000 for three years – and came in to opening day, no spring training or nothing, and got three hits. And, hey, he was a great outfielder. They didn't give him much credit for that. They always watched his hitting. Good fielder. Never threw to the wrong base. Like Ruth. He'd know the runners."

Wally Hebert, a pitcher for the St. Louis Browns in 1931 recalled pitching to Simmons in Tony Salin's 1999 book *Baseball's Forgotten Heroes.*

"…Al Simmons was the toughest guy with the A's," Hebert recalled, "I didn't know how to pitch against an opposite field hitting right-hander and that's what Al was. He'd step in to the bucket and hit it to right field. And I was pitching him right in his wheelhouse. I was pitching outside to him. I thought since he

The Duke of Milwaukee

was standing pretty far from the plate, I could pitch him outside. But he'd step in to the ball, you see, and he'd hit that opposite wall. I don't believe he ever hit a homerun off of me, but he hit the devil out of a couple of 'em against that wall in right field."

After the Major League Baseball season of 1931, Al joined several All-Stars and some members of the Philadelphia Athletics and began a tour of Hawaii and Japan. The tour, sponsored by *The Youmiuri Shimbun* one of Japan's leading newspapers, brought the American team to Meiji Shrine Stadium where in front of 65,000 rowdy fans paying upward of 40 yen (about $20), the U.S. team took the series opener by a score of 7-0. The American team was 17-0 on the trip.

Lou Gehrig on the First "Tour of Japan" club

Sportswriter Fred Lieb and businessman Herb Hunter co-managed the team that included pitchers Lefty Grove, Larry French and Bruce Cunningham, catchers Mickey Cochrane and Muddy Ruel, infielders Lou Gehrig (1b), Frankie Frisch (2b), Rabbit Maranville (ss) and Willie Kamm (3b). Joining Simmons in the outfield were Lefty O'Doul (who some call the "Father of Japanese professional baseball") and Tom Oliver. George Kelly and Ralph Shinners rounded out the playing roster as utility men.

Also making the trip were John Reardon, a big league umpire, and Dr. Leonard Knowles, who served as trainer.

The following year (1932), Yankee superstar, Lou Gehrig led a team of barnstormers to the Pacific in the name of competition and education. He commented to the New York Times, "the enthusiasm of the Japanese for baseball just about borders on fanatical." A team of interpreters followed the ballplayers to Japan's six leading universities so that the students, as well as Prince Chichibu of the royal family, could learn the intricacies of the game.

In 1934 Connie Mack and Babe Ruth headed baseball's most memorable "Tour of Japan" but despite a roster top heavy with A's players, Simmons (now with the White Sox) did not make the trip.

Al's life wasn't all baseball and like many other players of that era he was a big hunting and fishing fan. As soon as the season ended Al and his friends Mule Haas and Lefty Grove – and sometimes Mickey Cochrane – would head for the woods or a friendly Lake for some male bonding.

Most baseball writers thought that the A's would go for a fourth pennant in 1932 but, despite a generally good season, Mr. Mack's boys finished second, thirteen games behind Joe McCarthy's Yankees.

But on July 10, 1932 the A's visited the Cleveland Indians and what resulted was an incredible slug fest that saw the Mackmen triumph 18-17 in eighteen innings. Johnny Burnett, the Cleveland shortstop, got a major league record nine hits (in 11 trips to the plate) and the tribe totaled 33 hits – the A's 25. Eddie Rommel, the winning pitcher, gave up 29 hits in the 17 innings of

***Al was the cover boy for the
"Who's Who in Baseball" magazine***

The Duke of Milwaukee

relief that he worked. Lew Krausse started for the A's and lasted just one inning. Jimmie Foxx hit three homers (and six hits) for the A's, Simmons went five-for-nine and scored three. The game took four hours and five minutes to play.

For the year Al batted .322 with 35 homeruns and 151 RBI's – Foxx bashed 58 homers (and lost four others to rainouts) and Grove went 25-10. It would be the last time the A's ever finished this high.

Al's run with Philadelphia ended on September 28, 1932 and in a story by Gayle Talbot on the Associated Press wire dated September 29 the details of the deal unfolded.

Talbot wrote, "Connie Mack, venerable pilot of the Philadelphia Athletics has started tearing apart the great baseball machine he drove to three American League flags in 1929, '30 and '31, and the Chicago White Sox, at the time, have thrown their resources in to the market for players of proven ability.

"In one of the most startling deals of recent baseball history Manager Mack announced last night he had sold outfielders Al Simmons and George (Mule) Haas, and infielder Jimmy Dykes to the White Sox for cash.

"The price paid for the three stars was not announced but Sox officials said that it was the largest amount of cash they had ever handed out and probably the greatest sum which ever exchanged hands in the American League. It was estimated that the Sox put about $150,000 on the barrel head.

"Whether the sale presaged a general breaking up of the present Athletics team, Connie Mack would not say. The consensus was, however, that the 67-year-old leader had something of the sort in mind.

"Just 17 years ago he wrecked a glamorous team because it had become satiated with victory. At that time he sent one of his greatest stars, Eddie Collins, to the White Sox and Collins became the cornerstone of a championship team in Chicago.

"Where Mack contented himself with the bare announcement of the deal, Sox officials were less reticent.

"It means we are through trying to develop a winning team with rookies," said club secretary Harry Grabiner, "This is only the beginning. We are going out to get the players we want."

"While Haas and Dykes are considered valuable players, Simmons is the big gun in the deal. Possessed of a nine-year major league batting average of nearly .360, he is recognized as one of the game's greatest stars. He is one of the most feared batters in the big leagues, a ball hawk in left field, withal, a player any manager would welcome with open arms.

"He fell off in his hitting during the past season, finishing with an average around .323 but still is comparatively young and should prove a sound investment for the Sox. He was the batting champion of the American League in both 1930 and 1931.

"Opposing pitchers have feared him more than any batter in the Philadelphia constellation."

Two days later an article in *The Chicago Tribune* (dated October 1, 1932) stated "The last appearance of Al Simmons as a teammate of Jimmie Foxx and Mickey Cochrane of the Philadelphia Athletics is scheduled tomorrow at Borchert Field , Milwaukee, when the trio takes part in an exhibition game. Simmons will report to the Chicago White Sox next season.

"The exhibition tomorrow will start at 2.30 PM. Ten minutes before the game Simmons, Foxx and Cochrane will step to the plate to give a demonstration of the hitting prowess that enabled the trio to hit a collective total of 115 homeruns in the season just closed. Foxx rapped out 58, Simmons had 35, and Mickey 22.

"Assisting Simmons and his pals will be some of the leading minor league and Milwaukee stars. Bill Cissell of the Cleveland Indians will play shortstop for Foxx's team."

Some of the players included Ralph Blatz, Clary Hackbarth, Mandy Brooks, Abbe Eckert, Wacky Simmons (no relation to Al), Al Fons, Cuckoo Christensen and Tony Kubek Sr. (whose son would go on to have a fine career with the Yankees).

The Duke of Milwaukee

Chapter 4 – White Sox Years, 1933-35

Nationally known sportswriter Harold "Speed" Johnson writing in his landmark 1933 "Who's Who In Major League Baseball" said, "From sandlot to stardom well might describe the ascension of this larruping Polish athlete for he literally leaped off the prairie diamond of his beloved Milwaukee to immediately win renown as a fence buster. Now, following a brilliant career with the Athletics, we find him respondent in Chicago White Sox regimentals and still regarded as one of the game's most deadly hitters." (editor's note: They don't write like that anymore.)

1934 National Chicle baseball card shows Al with White Sox, card to left, 1933 Goudey gum card still has him in A's colors though it identifies him as playing for Chicago

When Al learned of his trade to the White Sox the Associated Press carried this story (Sept. 29, 1932).
"It's a good break for me".
In those few words, Al Simmons, Milwaukee's favorite ball player, voiced his opinion of the deal that sent him to Chicago.

The Duke of Milwaukee

"I hate to leave Connie Mack, but as long as he decided to sell me, I'm glad that he sent me to the White Sox.

"Chicago is one of the greatest baseball towns in the country. They have the greatest fans I've ever known. They've stuck with their ball club no matter where it finished. I'll be tickled to death to play there." In 1933 the Sox finished sixth under Lew Fonseca, but you couldn't blame Simmons. Al played in 145 games (he was just 31), batted .331, had 14 homeruns and 119 RBI's.

Early in the 1934 season, after his first four hits, Al reached 2,000 career hits, making him the fastest player to reach that plateau. That season the Chisox were dead last and Fonseca got fired after opening the season 4-13 and was replaced by 37-year-old third baseman Jimmy Dykes, who came to the Sox with Simmons at the close of the 1932 season. Al batted .344 in 138 games with 18 homeruns and 104 runs driven in. In fact, Al was pretty much the whole Chicago offense. Another former A's star, pitcher George "Moose" Earnshaw, paced the pitching department going 14-11.

In 1935 under Dykes the Pale Hose finished fifth, but Al had his worst season ever, hitting just .267 with 16 homers and 79 RBI's. He saw action 126 games.

1933 American League All-Stars

Al's White Sox years also included his only three appearances in an All-Star game (1933-35). He played centerfield in all three games, including the first one, under his old skipper Connie Mack, in 1933. Baseball's first All-Star Game, was held on July 6, 1933, at Chicago's Comiskey Park. It was the idea of Arch Ward, a sports editor for the Chicago Tribune, to coincide with the celebration of the city's "Century of Progress" Exposition. Baseball had established itself as America's favorite pastime and the national exposition provided the perfect stage to introduce baseball's best players to the rest of the country.

There were those who felt that a contest of this magnitude could not possibly live up to the fan's expectations, especially for those who lived in the far western states and had never been to a major league baseball game. The idea of a single game made up of the most exciting baseball-playing talent ever brought together on the diamond at one time, seemed too good to be true. Connie Mack, Al's old manager, piloted the 1933 club and Al played all nine innings. Both the 1933 and 1934, the All-Star teams were selected by the managers and the fans. The National League's manager, the now-retired, John McGraw and the American League's Connie Mack were chosen to pilot the first contest and to lead a line-up of big hitters including Lou Gehrig, Jimmie Foxx, Al Simmons and the one and only Babe Ruth. "We wanted to see the Babe," said Bill Hallahan, the National League starter. "Sure, he was old and had a big waistline, but that didn't make any difference. We were on the same field as Babe Ruth."

Babe Ruth hits first All-Star game homerun

The Duke of Milwaukee

With fellow All-Star, Charlie Gehringer on first in the bottom of the third, The Babe drove one into the right-field stands, the first homer in All-Star history. The crowd, according to one account, "roared in acclamation" and the first All-Star Game, won by the American League on the strength of Ruth's homer, was a resounding success.

Mr. Mack badly wanted to win this game over McGraw and, basically, stuck with his starters the whole way – Jimmie Foxx, Tony Lazzeri and Bill Dickey never got off the bench. Al, who started in center field and was 1-for-4 (a single to left in the fifth inning) moved over to left for the ninth inning. A's ace Lefty Grove pitched the last three innings.

The second All-Star game was held on July 10 at the New York Polo Grounds. Joe Cronin managed the American League, Bill Terry was the National League's pilot. Once again, the batting line-up featured some of the best hitters in baseball. This game however, belonged to a pitcher, Carl Hubbell. Although he started off poorly, he turned in perhaps one of the most spellbinding performances ever seen in baseball.

First, Charlie Gehringer led off with a single and moved to second on an outfield error. Then, Heinie Manush drew a walk bringing up Babe Ruth, Lou Gehrig and Jimmie Foxx with two on, none out. It was a pitcher's worst nightmare. Hubbell accepted the challenge and began turning over his screwball with pinpoint precision. It was a delivery that was designed to break the backs of free swingers. Ruth was the first to fall after taking a called third strike and looking "decidedly puzzled," according to one account. Gehrig followed and went down swinging. Visibly frustrated, he apparently warned Foxx on his way back to the dugout, "You might as well cut. It won't get any higher." The advice didn't help; Foxx went down on strikes. In the second inning, Hubbell made it five in a row when he struck out Al Simmons and Joe Cronin. If the first All-Star Game had showcased the game's best bats, then the second showcased one of the games best arms proving that both offense and defense had a place in the Midsummer Classic.

When the game ended, though, the American League had made it two-in-a-row with a 9-7 victory. Al went 3-for-5 and scored three runs. He also had an RBI. Again he started in centerfield and then moved over to left. He had now played every inning of the first two All-Star contests. Mel Harder was the winning pitcher.

Donald Honig wrote, "Simmons was a testy character who was called 'a 'swashbuckling pirate of a man' by one contemporary. King of his league's right-handed hitters for a decade, he was an elitist who bullied rookies, manifested a chilly disdain for lesser mortals and even, on occasion, questioned the wisdom of Connie Mack"

In August, 1934, Al married Doris Lynn Reader and they had a son, John Alan. The marriage did not last and they were later divorced. Because of religious convictions (Al was a Catholic, his wife was Jewish) he never re-married and remained a lonely man until he died.

Al's son was proud of his father, according to Greaber, but he never really got to spend much time with him. "John Alan, who they called 'The Little Duke' after Al, spent his school years in boarding schools – when Al was not playing ball – and in the summer's he would always spend a couple of weeks with Al wherever he played (or coached)."

Greaber said that Little Duke was never interested in sports, "most likely because baseball cost him precious time with his father. He spent a lot of time vying for his father's attention and trying to live up to being the son of a celebrity."

Al once told a friend, "Mr. Mack seemed to look on me as his son. He never stopped feeling sorry for me after the break-up of my marriage." According to published reports Mr. Mack tried to get Al and Doris to try and work things out after the divorce, but without success.

Al's last All-Star appearance came on July 8, 1935 in Cleveland's Municipal Stadium as 69,831 spectators watched. Mickey Cochrane, the Tigers skipper, managed the AL, Frankie Frisch of the Cardinals was the NL pilot. Simmons went 2-for-4 playing centerfield. He didn't finish the game though as Roger "Doc" Cramer came in to replace him late in the contest. The AL won again, 4-1, and Lefty Gomez pitched the first six innings.

The American League actually won for the third straight year due to the performance of Jimmie Foxx. Foxx was playing third in deference to Lou Gehrig and belted a two-run homer in

The Duke of Milwaukee

the bottom of the first, giving the junior circuit a lead it never relinquished. Making his third All-Star appearance, Simmons was the game's top hitter with a six-for-thirteen showing and a .462 average. Ironically it would be his last All-Star showing. Unbelievably, the most frustrated hitter was Gehrig. A Triple Crown winner in 1934, he was hitless in nine at-bats in three games.

The Duke of Milwaukee

Chapter 5 – A Year as a Tiger, Two with the Nats

It was only one year, a brief reunion with his old pal from the A's gravy days – and his skipper in the '35 All-Star game, Detroit Tigers manager Mickey Cochrane. The defending AL champion Tigers bought Al for $75,000 over the winter and before the next season he was to move again.

Photo courtesy of Al Simmons Family – Patrick Greaber
Al, Mickey Cochrane and Cy Perkins reunited in Detroit

To all intents and purposes Al did what was asked of him, in fact he even played first base in one game. He was batting .350 lifetime when he went to the Bengals, and for them he played in 143 games, batted .327, hit 13 homers and drove in 112 runs. He had clearly recovered from whatever ailed him in Chicago the year before. The Tigers finished second but were 19-and-a-half games out of first behind the Yankees.

35

The Duke of Milwaukee

Reading between the lines of press reports of the day, Al's attitude was becoming a problem and he wasn't taking very good care of himself. So, even though he had solid numbers, he was dispatched to Washington for the next season.

Al had done well statistically in Detroit in 1936, but the Tigers decided to unload him and sold his contract to the Washington Senators for $15,000. Imagine.

Al spent two years with the Nationals

Al had never been popular with the Washington fans – much in the same way that Philadelphia Phillies fans once jeered Pete Rose as a member of the Reds – but owner Clark Griffith felt that Al might be just the ticket to get the Senators back to the World Series.

Joe Cronin had led them to the promised land in 1933, but by 1934 they were back in seventh place. In 1935 the one-time "Boy Wonder" manager Bucky Harris was back at the helm (he had guided the Nats to the pennant in 1924 and 1925).

When Al heard the news he was quoted in the press as saying "It certainly suits me, and it looks like a great place for me. I think the Washington club is going places."

As the mid-to-late1930's played out, Griffith was clearly building for the future and felt that a seasoned veteran and lifetime .300 hitter might be just what the club needed. But it soon became clear that if they going any place clearly Al wasn't going to take them there.

The Duke of Milwaukee

In 1937 the Senators finished sixth (73-80) and Al he appeared in just 103 games – the lowest number since he became a regular with the A's in 1924. He batted just .279 only the second time in his career he had hit below .300. He drove in 84 runs and had just eight homeruns. It was a long season marked by illness and the fact that Simmons was not in the best playing shape.

In 1938 it didn't get a lot better for Washington. They moved up a notch to fifth place (75-76) and Al appeared in 125 games, got his average back over .300 (at .302), hit 21 homers and drove in 95. He was 36 years old.

While with the Senators Al befriended young outfielder George Case, who would go on to fine career in the majors. One evening in a Boston bar Al asked Case to join him for a drink. With no game the next day, the two men drank together until 2.30 AM, the tee totaling Case drinking ginger ale while Al indulged in his drink of choice, Scotch and water.

Simmons told Case the story of his life-to-date, saying, "You know I have a reputation for being coarse and a little ornery, but believe me, enough things have happened to me in my life to account for that." He told Case of his childhood, how poor the family was, and how hard he had to work when he was a lad.

After that evening the two outfielders became close friends and Simmons gave the young man a lot of good advice and encouragement. Later in life Case recalled Al and said, "He turned out to be, under that gruff exterior, a very kind and thoughtful man."

But considering what Case thought of him, on the last day of the '38 season Al managed to talk himself out of the nation's capitol. He got in to a row with the fans after they had taunted him mercilessly. In fact during his final at-bat he challenged three fans to meet him, after the game, under the stands. He issued a second, then a third, challenge and, finally, dispatched the clubhouse boy with a note.

Griffith freaked out. "No ballplayer of mine can conduct himself in such a manner," he said. He then announced that he was fining Simmons $200 and was going to report him the

The Duke of Milwaukee

American League President Will Harridge and Commissioner Judge Kenesaw Mountain Landis.

Continuing his rant to the press, Griffith said, "The language displayed by Simmons was not only objectionable, but obscene."

Al came back at Griffith and claimed that the fine was the boss's way of recapturing most of the $300 bonus promised to him if he batted over .300.

Ironically the three young men that Simmons had threatened said it was a case of mistaken identity and the real culprit was a man sitting several rows behind them. Later Simmons admitted he wasn't sure who had been riding him, "but I don't agree with people who say a fan is entitled to call a player any name he chooses."

Honig said, "Simmons with his boiling hatred of pitchers and a lifetime batting average of .334 is becoming a statue in a dark and unvisited basement."

On December 29, 1938 Al's contract was purchased by the Boston Bees for $3,000 and he was on his way to the National League and would get to play in one more World Series.

Chapter 6 – Al Shifts to the National League, Chases 3000 hits

John P. Carmichael of the *Chicago Daily News* and editor of *Who's Who In The Major Leagues* wrote "The Duke of Milwaukee may be getting along in years, but an undimmed eye keeps him up there in the gilded tower among the .350 hitters. For fifteen years he has averaged this 18-karat figure – nine with the Athletics, three with the White Sox, one with the Tigers and the last two with the Nationals. Now he hits Boston, and *how* he hits."

Al as a Boston Bee

It was just three seasons earlier that another aging American League slugger, Babe Ruth, ended up on the Boston Bees roster and that didn't work out so terribly well. And, sadly, neither did Simmons' tenure in Beantown.

The Bees were ahead of only the lowly Phillies in the NL standings when they dealt Simmons to the league leading Cincinnati Reds on August 31. The did Al a favor and got him in to his fourth World's Series. Al batted .282 in 82 games for the Bees, but managed just seven homers and 43 ribbies.

When he joined the Reds it was strictly as an insurance policy and he saw action in just nine games – five as an outfielder – and managed just three hits in 21 plate appearances.

The Duke of Milwaukee

His average was an atrocious .143. One of his teammates on the '39 Reds was Eddie Joost, with whom he would be reunited in 1947 with the A's when Connie Mack rescued the shortstop from the minors and embarked on, what many thought would be, one last run at the championship.

1939 NL Champion Reds - Al is 4th from left, second row

Bill McKechnie's Reds went down in four straight to the mighty Yankees, but Al did see action in one game as an outfielder and went 1-for-4.

As Al grew older getting 3,000 hits became an obsession with him and he played longer than he should have.

In 1940 he appeared in 37 games for the A's and got 25 hits. In 1941 he saw action in just nine games and managed just three more. He spent 1942 as a coach, but when World War II opened the game up for older (and much younger) players Al saw one last opportunity and signed on with the Boston Red Sox. It didn't work. He played in just 40 games and got 27 more hits.

The Duke of Milwaukee

Back with the A's for one last try, Al gave it up in mid-summer after getting three hits in just six at bats. His final number was 2,927 – he missed it by 73 hits.

Looking back on his career Al lamented the times he had begged off playing to nurse a hang-over or when he asked out of a one-sided game for a quick shower and an early start for a night on the town.

In five of his seasons as a regular he played in 125 or fewer games – of a 154 game season. Think of the hits he could have gotten had he played in close to the full schedule of games.

In the 1940's Al met a young player of Polish heritage like his own and told Stan Musial, "Never relax on any time at bat; never miss a game you can play." Musial took it to heart, apparently, rapping out 3,630 hits over his long career with the Cardinals.

The Duke of Milwaukee

Al in West Palm Beach in 1949 for his last spring Training with the A's

Chapter 7– The 1940's..Al's Years as a Coach

"Coaching third base is the toughest job on the ball club," Simmons once said. "The coach gets all the blame when things go wrong and a runner gets thrown out at the plate and none of the credit when things go right"

It may have been a tough job but Al was good at it and handled the job for a number of years for his mentor, Connie Mack, beginning in 1940 wearing the dual title of player-coach.

Player Simmons got in to 37 games for the A's in 1940 and batted .309 – the man could still hit but his body wasn't as willing as it once had been. But the following year he was, mostly, a coach appearing in just nine games and hitting .125.

By 1942 he was strictly Coach Simmons, working the hot corner coaching box with efficiency.

Dom DiMaggio and "Catfish" Metkovich

The Duke of Milwaukee

But World War II broke out and good players (and those whose names would actually sell tickets) were in short supply – especially those with lifetime batting averages well over .300 – and so Al signed on as a player with the Boston Red Sox. He was out of shape, 41-years-of-age and got in to 40 games with 141 plate appearances and managed just 27 hits – one of them a homerun. His batting average was a scandalous (for Al) .203. It must have killed him to sit on the bench and watch the Red Sox field everyday outfielders named Pete Fox, George "Catfish" Metkovich and Leon Culberson. The Red Sox finished in seventh place under Joe Cronin who was 36 and also playing.

It is likely that Al connected with the Bosox due to his friendship with their star centerfielder Dom DiMaggio – who was in the service during Al's brief stay in Beantown. Al was also friendly with Dom's older brother Vince.

Joe Planamente, a member of the Philadelphia Athletics Historical Society, writing in the club's *Along the Elephant Trail* newsletter recalled when Al Simmons hit a home run "just for him".

Joe said that he was always an Al Simmons fan but never got to see him play until 1937 when he was with Washington and "..his career was going down hill.."

In 1943 Planamente was in the Navy and assigned to "boot camp" in Samson, N.Y. The Red Sox scheduled an exhibition game there against the base team and Joe paid another sailor to take his "watch" so he could see the game.

"As luck would have it," Joe recalled, "the game was called after just three innings due to rain. Now I made up my mind to go talk to 'Bucket foot Al' and I did so. When I approached him he was stuffing his gear in an old canvas bag.

"I introduced myself and told him that I was from Philadelphia. He shook his head and said, 'Ah, Philly, my happiest days were playing in Philly.

"I told him that I had rooted for him as a kid and he told me he thought that was great. He added, 'well kid, I wish you luck, take care of yourself' and with that he got on the bus and when he was seated I said to him, "Al can't you get those last few hits to reach 300? He stared at me with a sad look and said,

'I don't think so, I'm only up here for a cup of coffee.' I knew what he meant, he was only playing because of the war.

"As the bus started moving I ran along side and, like a kid, I yelled 'Al, Al how about hitting a homer for me this season?' This time a smile crossed his face and he pointed a finger at me and said, 'Kid, the first one this year is for you!'

"In 1943 Al Simmons hit just one homerun and it was the last homerun of his illustrious career. You could look it up."

Al was released at the end of the season and would return to the A's signing on as a free agent on April 15, 1944 – opening day. Again he was a player-coach, but mostly a coach, and appeared in just four games, getting three hits in six trips to the plate, all as a pinch hitter.

Spring Training 1947 – Coach Al with, left to right, Mason Bowes, Joe Astroth and Leon Griffith

Officially released as a player the following season, Al stayed with the A's as a coach until the close of the 1949 season.

Bill Hockenbury, a Philadelphia area native, who spent nine seasons in the minors – most in the A's farm system – recalls Simmons with great affection.

The Duke of Milwaukee

Hockenbury went to spring training with the big club in 1947 and remembers Simmons working with him. "I was told that Al was one of my biggest boosters," Bill recalls.

Originally a switch-hitter Hockenbury was told to bat just right-handed and, in hindsight, feels that while it may have boosted his power numbers but it probably took 50 points off my batting average and, as a third baseman, if you didn't hit both with power and for the numbers you didn't stick in those days.

"Simmons told me not to let them mess with my swing," Hockenbury recalled, "but I was young and I did what I was told. I remember Al saying 'they tried to mess with my swing too when I first came up but I wouldn't let them' and I should have listened."

"Al really told it like it was," Bill laughed, "he shot from the hip. He was really quite a down-to-earth man."

Hockenbury remembers Al as being "the most liked of all Mr. Mack's coaches" and thinks that his popularity may have ultimately cost him his job.

In a move that caught A's fans by surprise Al and Earle Brucker Sr., two of Mr. Mack's most trusted and highly regarded coaches were dismissed in October 1949 by Mack's youngest son, Connie Jr., as the unwitting victims of a family struggle for control of the ball club.

In making the announcement of Al's dismissal Mr. Mack, with tears in his eyes, said that it wasn't his decision but rather one made by the club's board of directors. When Connie was actually in control of the ball club he'd have told the "board of directors" that he wasn't having any of it...and wouldn't have.

1949 Coaching Staff – Earle Mack, Earl Brucker, Mr. Mack, Al Simmons and Jimmy Dykes

The Duke of Milwaukee

The stories persist that Al really managed the A's frequently during the mid-40's when Mr. Mack was either physically indisposed or simply not alert enough to do it. Stories actually appeared in the press speculating that Simmons, not Mack's son Earle, would ultimately succeed him and that, too, may have played a part in his demise with the A's. Feedback that I've gotten from other ex-A's over the year painted Earle as something of a laughing stock among the players and that no one seriously believed that Mr. Mack would ever turn the club over to Earle when he finally retired. And, of course, he didn't.

Connie Jr. was apparently unaware of a promise his father had made to Simmons when Al returned to the club in 1944. Mr. Mack told Al that "there will always be a place for you in the Philadelphia organization."

As the story goes, Al thanked Mr. Mack for his assurance and then pointed out that Mr. Mack wouldn't always be around to guarantee it. Mack took it in stride and said, "I think my sons know how I feel about it." Simmons, still not convinced, said, "Maybe they do, but would you mind telling them?"

Apparently he didn't.

When he was released by the A's he said, "Baseball doesn't owe me a thing. It was wonderful to me, and I owe everything I've got to the game. That's one reason why I'd like to stay with it. No other business or fame could have given me so many happy years."

A newspaper photo of Al in his Indians attire

The Duke of Milwaukee

Lou Boudreau, who'd be entering his final season as skipper of the Cleveland Indians, gave him a chance to stay with it and signed Al to be his third base coach for 1950. Despite winning 92 games, but finishing fourth, Boudreau was canned. New manager Al Lopez invited Simmons to remain on the staff for 1951 but after taking ill in spring training Al was released and replaced by Red Ruffing on the coaching lines.

His days in uniform and in organized baseball had come to an end.

Chapter 8 – The Hall of Fame

Some years ago a member of the Philadelphia Athletics Historical Society passed along a letter to me that Al Simmons had written to a sportswriter friend of his in 1951.

Al, who was then ill and out of baseball and living at the Milwaukee Athletic Club, was feeling down in the dumps and unappreciated. He had, again, been overlooked by the BBWAA getting 51.3% of the vote.

In his letter Al begged the man to "get behind me" for inclusion in to the Hall of Fame – an amazing plea considering that his statistics ranked him among baseball's best – and a terrible indictment of the favoritism shown by baseball writers of that time who, in 1947 his first year of eligibility had virtually snubbed him giving him just 3.7% of the vote.

He failed to gain induction in 1952 (60.3%) but in 1953 he finally joined the elite with 75.4% of the ballots cast in his favor. Also inducted in 1953 were Umpires Bill Klem and Tom Connolly, Pitchers Chief Bender and Dizzy Dean and Executive Ed Barrow.

Jimmie Foxx had been inducted in 1951 and his teammates from A's championship years – Mickey Cochrane and Lefty Grove had been in since 1947.

His career stats were certainly worthy of Cooperstown. He hit over .300 thirteen times (in 20 seasons), twice was the top batter in the AL (1930 with a .381 average and 1931 when he batted .390) and finished with a lifetime batting mark of .334. He stroked 307 homeruns and drove in 1,827. He appeared in four World Series, batting .329 in 19 games with six homeruns. He also appeared in three All-Star games.

Al's acceptance speech at his induction was one of humility. He devoted little time to his own career and spent most of his talk paying tribute to his friend, mentor, and some say surrogate father, Connie Mack.

Ralph "Cy" Perkins, a longtime A's teammate and, later, a coach with the Philadelphia Phillies summed up Al's career when he spoke of him on induction day at Cooperstown. "He had the swagger of confidence, of defiance, when he came up as a kid. He was sensational as a rookie as he was as a star. I've always classed him next to Ty Cobb (Simmons' idol) as the greatest player I ever saw. He was what I could call "the perfect player".

ALOYSIUS HARRY SIMMONS
PLAYED WITH 7 MAJOR LEAGUE CLUBS 1924-1944. STAR WITH PHILA.(A.L.). BATTED .308 TO .392 FROM 1924 TO 1934. LEADING BATTER .381 IN 1930, .390 IN 1931. MOST HITS BY A.L. RIGHT-HANDED BATTER WITH 2831. LED LEAGUE RUNS BATTED IN, RUNS SCORED, HITS AND TOTAL BASES SEVERAL SEASONS. HIT 3 HOME RUNS, JULY 15, 1932. LIFETIME BATTING AVERAGE .334.

Al's Plaque in Cooperstown

 Sportswriter Bob Broeg wrote of Perkins' platitudes "High praise indeed, and even when he began to spend too much time with the sauce (drinking) in his last professional job as a coach with the Cleveland Indians in 1950, Simmons took great pride in proper techniques and methods."
 Often forgotten is the fact that Al was an outstanding outfielder. In 5,251 chances over his 20-year-career Al made but 94 errors and boasted a .982 fielding average. He played one game at first base and fielded 12 chances flawlessly.
 Though Al played for several teams in the majors his plaque in Cooperstown shows him in his familiar A's cap.

The Duke of Milwaukee

In his last years in baseball Mr. Mack reflected on his long career and, strangely, kept just one picture of a ball player in his office. That player was Al Simmons. When asked which of all his players could provide the most value for a team, the legendary manager reportedly said, "If only I could have nine players named Al Simmons."

Greaber, talking about the memorabilia that Al left for his family, says "we found several player contracts that he never signed. He was always a difficult player to sign." (His notorious 1931 hold-out resulted in his $100,000 three-year contract. He missed all of spring training that year and then signed and was in the starting lineup on opening day.)

Other family treasures include a pocket watch, tie tack and a ring, each commemorating one of the three championships the A's won between 1929 and 1931.

In 2000 Al was named to the Athletics "All 20th Century" team – filling an outfield that included Reggie Jackson and Rickey Henderson. He is often referred to as the best athlete to ever come out of Wisconsin.

The Duke of Milwaukee

Chapter 9 – The Twilight Years

Some say Al was heartbroken when, after the 1949 season, the Philadelphia A's fired him and fellow longtime coach Earle Brucker Sr.

Irony played a part. It was Connie Mack who brought him to the majors – and the Athletics – and it was Connie Mack Jr., locked in a power struggle for control of the A's with his older brothers, who spelled the end of Simmons' tenure with the club.

The younger Connie, in winning the first round of the power struggle, got older brother Earle to retire as assistant manager (despite the fact that Connie Mack states in his, obviously ghost-written 1950 book, that Earle would succeed him as manager) and secured the dismissal of both Simmons and Brucker who were seen as the last remnants of that regime.

1949 Philadelphia Athletics – Al's Last A's team

Earle Mack and his brother Roy would ultimately prevail in their long battle – consenting to allow their father to manage "as long as he wants to" – in exchange for the rights to buy Connie Jr.'s stock and that held by his mother and members of the Shibe/McFarland families.

This ill-forged deal would cost the city the franchise after the 1954 season. Roy Mack accompanied the team to Kansas City in pretty much a ceremonial vice president's role, while

The Duke of Milwaukee

Earle never worked another day in baseball. Roy resigned from the KC A's after one season.

To replace Simmons they brought in another Hall of Famer, Mickey Cochrane, and some sportswriter's saw the one-time Tigers manager as Mack's successor. Cochrane was given the title of general manager/coach. Insiders, on the other hand, would concede that Cochrane was never the same after his near-tragic beaning over a decade before and that he was brought in because he posed no threat at all to the Earle-Roy Mack management team. In Cochrane's declining years, it was later revealed, that Ty Cobb had kept him from poverty by paying most, if not all, of his bills.

Lou Boudreau, Cleveland manager

Lou Boudreau, the one-time "Boy Wonder" skipper of the Cleveland Indians added Simmons to his coaching staff for 1950 and he donned #44 and worked the third base coaching box for the rival AL club. Boudreau's tenure as chief of the tribe ended at the close of the season.

Slated to return in 1951 Simmons showed up in spring training in terrible physical shape, was drinking to excess, and generally was in poor health. New manager Al Lopez wanted nothing or no one on his team that would distract the players from the rebuilding program then going in to effect and Al was quietly asked to resign.

Al returned to Milwaukee an unhappy man but struggled to maintain a reason for being – he was, after all, only 49. He got involved in the local sand lot baseball program for the next few years telling people that he wanted to help other kids with the same kind of program in which he got his start.

On May 26, 1956 Al collapsed on the sidewalk outside of the Milwaukee Athletic Club where he resided. He was dead-on-arrival at the hospital. Death was attributed to a heart attack.

Simmons had turned 54 four days before. Connie Mack had preceded him in death by three months. He was buried in St. Adalbert's Cemetery in Milwaukee.

Al's son, John Alan Simmons, a retired Air Force captain passed away on January 30, 2010 at the age of 74, he was a resident of Atlanta, GA and also maintained a home in Guadeloupe, Mexico.

While never an athlete, John Alan's career of service to his country included flying rescue missions during the Vietnam War. He suffered from Multiple Sclerosis later in life and found the weather in Mexico to be better for his health. His son-in-law said his disposition was similar to Al's and he was a very private person. John Alan was just 20 when Al Simmons died.

He was preceded in death by his son David, who died quite young in an accident, and is survived by daughter Karen Greaber and son Daniel. He also was survived by granddaughters Alison Simmons and Madison Greaber.

John Alan's son Daniel is called a "dead ringer" for Al by Patrick Greaber and he mentions that Al's genes were passed down to his wife Karen "who was an outstanding softball player in high school, in fact she got college scholarship offers."

John Alan's half sister, Heidi Waldman also survives.

The Duke of Milwaukee

Chapter 10 – Al Simmons's Amazing Stats

Al Simmons was truly an amazing player as the following statistics will show you. His big league playing career lasted 20 years, but he was in a big league uniform for close to 26 seasons.

He played under some great, some good and, perhaps, one not-so-good managers. Awards and honors accrued to him throughout his lifetime – and beyond.

The Duke of Milwaukee

Al Simmons career as a player

Year – Team

Minor Leagues	G	BA	AB	H	Hr	RBI
1922 – Aberdeen (D)	118	.348	445	155	11	n/a
1922 – Milwaukee (AA)	19	.220	50	11	1	n/a
1923 – Shreveport (A)	99	.360	525	189	12	n/a
1923 – Milwaukee (AA)	24	.398	98	39	0	n/a
Major Leagues						
1924 – Philadelphia A's	152	.308	594	183	8	102
1925 – Philadelphia A's	153	.387	654	253	24	129
1926 – Philadelphia A's	147	.341	583	199	19	109
1927 – Philadelphia A's	106	.392	406	159	15	108
1928 – Philadelphia A's	119	.351	464	163	15	107
1929 – Philadelphia A's	143	.365	581	212	34	157
1930 – Philadelphia A's	138	.381	554	211	36	165
1931 – Philadelphia A's	128	.390	513	200	22	128
1932 – Philadelphia A's	154	.322	670	216	35	151
1933 – Chicago White Sox	146	.331	605	200	14	119
1934 – Chicago White Sox	138	.344	558	192	18	104
1935 – Chicago White Sox	128	.267	525	140	16	79
1936 – Detroit Tigers	143	.327	568	186	13	112
1937 – Washington Senators	103	.279	419	117	8	84
1938 – Washington Senators	125	.302	470	142	21	95
1939 – Boston Bees	93	.282	330	93	7	43
Cincinnati Reds	9	.143	21	3	0	1
1940 – Philadelphia A's	37	.309	81	25	1	19
1941 – Philadelphia A's	9	.125	24	3	0	1
1943 – Boston Red Sox	40	.203	133	27	1	12
1944 – Philadelphia A's	4	.500	6	3	0	2

Major League Lifetime

20 seasons	2215	.334	8759	2927	307	1827

Post Season (World Series)

Year – team	G	BA	AB	H	HR	RBI
1929 – Philadelphia A's	5	.300	20	6	2	5
1930 – Philadelphia A's	6	.364	22	8	2	4
1931 – Philadelphia A's	7	.333	27	9	2	8
1939 – Cincinnati Reds	1	.250	4	1	0	0
4 seasons	19	.329	73	24	6	17

Statistical Leader

1925 – Leads AL in at-bats with 654 and hits with 253
1929 – Leads AL in RBI's with 157
1930 – Leads AL in batting with .381 average and most runs with 152
1931 – Leads AL in batting with .390 average.
1932 – Leads AL in at-bats with 670 and hits with 216.

Honors

1929 – Most Valuable Player, American League. Voted by *The Sporting News.*
1933, 34, 35 – Named to the American League All-Star team
1951 – Elected to Wisconsin Athletic Hall of Fame
1953 – Inducted in to the Baseball Hall of Fame
2000 – Named to the Athletics All 20th Century team

Al's baseball transactions

December 15, 1923 – A's acquire Al Simmons from the minor league Milwaukee Brewers for players Wid Mathews, Beauty McGowan and Heine Scheer and $40,00 cash.

September 28, 1932 – A's trade Al Simmons, Jimmy Dykes and Mule Haas to the Chicago White Sox for $100,000.

December 10, 1935 – Al Simmons sold to the Detroit Tigers by the Chicago White Sox for $75,000.

April 4, 1937 – Washington Senators purchase Al Simmons from Detroit for $15,000.

December 29, 1938 – Al Simmons is sold to the Boston Bees for $3,000.

August 31, 1939 – Cincinnati Reds purchase Al Simmons from Boston for an undisclosed cash price.

October 19, 1939 – Al Simmons is released outright by Cincinnati.

December 8, 1939 – Al Simmons signs with the A's as a free agent.

February 2, 1943 – Al Simmons signs with the Boston Red Sox as a free agent after the A's give him his release so that he can sign on elsewhere as a player. He is released at the end of the season.

April 15, 1944 – Al Simmons signs with the Philadelphia A's as a free agent.

The Duke of Milwaukee

June 15, 1945 – Al Simmons is released as a player and signed as a coach by the Philadelphia A's.

October 15, 1949 – Al Simmons and Earle Brucker Sr. are released as coaches by the A's. He signs on with Cleveland as a coach.

March 30, 1951 – Al Simmons is released as a coach by the Indians in Spring Training due to ill health.

Career Batting Average Leaders

Al stands 21st among all-time career batting leaders. This slot places him ahead of such super stars as Sam Thompson (.331), Stan Musial (.331), Cap Anson (.329), Honus Wagner (.327), Earle Combs (.325), Joe DiMaggio (.325), Jimmie Foxx (.325), Babe Herman (.324), kiKi Cuyler (.321), Pie Traynor (.320), Mickey Cochrane (.320), Charlie Gehringer (.320) and Chuck Klein (.320) in the top 50.

Player	Yrs	G	AB	H	BA
1. Ty Cobb	24	3035	11343	4189	.366
2. Rogers Hornsby	23	2259	8173	2930	.358
3. Joe Jackson	13	1332	4981	1772	.356
4. Ed Delahanty	16	1835	7505	2596	.346
5. Tris Speaker	22	2789	10195	3514	.345
6. Billy Hamilton	14	1591	6268	2158	.344
7. Ted Williams	19	2291	7706	2654	.344
8. Dan Brothers	19	1673	6711	2296	.342
9. Harry Heilmann	17	2148	7787	2660	.342
10. Babe Ruth	22	2503	8399	2873	.342
11. Bill Terry	14	1721	6428	2193	.341
12. Pete Browning	13	1183	4820	1646	.341
13. Willie Keeler	19	2123	8591	2932	.341
14. Lou Gehrig	17	2164	8001	2721	.340
15. George Sisler	15	2055	8267	2812	.340
16. Tony Gwynn	20	2440	9288	3141	.338
17. Jesse Burkett	16	2066	8421	2850	.338
18. Nap Lajoie	21	2480	9589	3242	.338
19. Riggs Stephenson	14	1310	4508	1515	.336
20. John J. McGraw	16	1099	3924	1309	.334
21. AL SIMMONS	20	2215	8759	2927	.334
22. Eddie Collins, 23. Mike Donlin and 24. Paul Waner all tied at					.333

The Duke of Milwaukee

Career Hit Leaders

Al Simmons stands 35th among all-time hit leaders. He will drop to 36th in 2011 after Derek Jeter collects two base hits. He stood 13th All-Time when he retired in 1944. List as of 1/1/2011

1. Pete Rose	4256
2. Ty Cobb	4189
3. Hank Aaron	3771
4. Stan Musial	3630
5. Tris Speaker	3514
6. Cap Anson	3435
7. Honus Wagner	3420
8. Carl Yastzremski	3419
9. Paul Molitor	3319
10. Eddie Collins	3311
11. Willie Mays	3283
12. Eddie Murray	3255
13. Larry Lajoie	3242
14. Cal Ripken Jr.	3184
15. George Brett	3154
16. Paul Waner	3152
17. Robin Yount	3142
18. Tony Gwynn	3141
19. Dave Winfield	3110
20. Craig Biggio	3060
21. Rickey Henderson	3055
22. Rod Carew	3053
23. Lou Brock	3023
24. Rafael Palmeiro	3020
25. Wade Boggs	3010
26. Al Kaline	3007
27. Roberto Clemente	3000
28. Sam Rice	2987
29. Sam Crawford	2961
30. Frank Robinson	2943
31. Barry Bonds	2935
32. Jake Beckley	2934
33. Willie Keeler	2932
34. Rogers Hornsby	2930
35. AL SIMMONS	2927
36. Derek Jeter	2926

The Duke of Milwaukee

Al Simmons' uniform numbers

**1924-30, Philadelphia Athletics didn't wear numbers, from 1931-36 they only wore them on the road
1931 – Philadelphia Athletics #7
1932 – Philadelphia Athletics #7
1933 - Chicago White Sox #5
1934 –35 Chicago White Sox #7
1936 – Detroit Tigers #6
1937 – Washington Senators #3
1938 – Washington Senators #7
1939 – Boston Braves #20
1939 – Cincinnati Reds #38
1940 – Philadelphia Athletics #6
1941 –42 Philadelphia Athletics #28
1943 – Boston Red Sox #8
1944 –49 Philadelphia Athletics #32 (coach)
1950 – Cleveland Indians #44 (coach)**

The Duke of Milwaukee

Charles "Casey' Stengel

Joe Cronin

Managers that Al played/Coached for

1924-32, 40-42, 44-49 Connie Mack, A's
1933, Lou Fonseca, White Sox
1934, Fonseca & Jimmy Dykes, White Sox
1935, Jimmy Dykes, White Sox

1936, Mickey Cochrane, Tigers
1937-38, Bucky Harris, Senators
1939, Casey Stengel, Boston NL
1939, Bill McKechnie, Reds
1943, Joe Cronin, Boston AL
1950, Lou Boudreau, Indians

The Duke of Milwaukee

Chapter 11 – Al Simmons Collectibles

Autographs –

Signed in 1949 for a fan

Al Simmons was an obliging signer and, though he died suddenly at age 54, his signature is still reasonably available to diligent collectors.
Sports Collectors Digest suggests that you'll pay $250 for a cut, $350 for a signed 3x5 card, $1,000 for a signed photo, $5,000 for a single signed ball (less if on a late 40's multi-signed team ball when he was a coach).

Baseball Cards –

There are many Simmons cards in the market place according to the *Beckett Alphabetical Baseball Card checklist book*. The earliest was a 1926 Sporting News card, Exhibit cards (1923, 1928, 1933), U. S. Caramel, Delong, Tattoo Orbit, Goudey, National Chicle and various A's club issues in the 40's. He also appeared on many cards after he passed including the 1960 Fleer set, the Conlin Collection cards and various Topps, Fleer, Upper Deck old-timer issues.

One omission escapes logic. In 1939, 40 and 41 the Philadelphia based Gum, Inc. issued their fairly large "Play Ball" sets and even though Al was active in two of the three years – and the 1940, especially, was loaded with old-timers – Al did not appear on a card. A second omission would be by the Exhibit

The Duke of Milwaukee

Supply Co. which issued "Hall of Fame" sets in 1948 and 1977 – and skipped him both times.

Values of some of the older cards include:
1923 – Exhibit card #50 $125
1926 – Sporting News card #8 $160
1927 – W560, card #39 $55
1928 – Exhibit card #49 $100
1931 – W-UNC Strip cards #15 $75

1927 W-560 Baseball card

1933 – Delong, card #2 $575
1933 – Goudey, card #35 $600
1933 – Tattoo Orbit #53 $160

1931 W-517 Baseball card

1931 – W517, card #40 $150
1932 – U. S. Caramel, card #17 $600
1933 – Butter Creams, card #24 $600
1933 – Exhibit cards (4-on-1) w/Cochrane, Foxx and Grove, $250

1933 Tattoo Orbit baseball card

1933 – Rittenhouse candy, card #40 $130
1933 – Worch Cigar card #118 $80
1934 – Butterfinger, card #W55 $115
1934 – Batter-Up, card #34 $200

1934 – W574 card #126 $125
1934-36 – Diamond Stars, card #2 (each year), $465
1935 – Wheaties – Series 1, card #25 $60
1936 – World Wide Gum (Canadian Goudey) card #77 $225
1936 – Goudey "Wide Pen" card #147 $50
1936 – National Chicle "Fine Pen" card #96 $50
1939 – Goudey Premiums, card #40 $135
1949 – Fun Book, Phila. Sunday Bulletin
1950 – Callahan Hall of Fame set, card #65 $20

Many baseball cards were issued after Al died in 1956 – and are still being issued today. Some of the more significant include:

1960 – Fleer, card #32 $15
1961 – Fleer, card #77 $15
1974 – TCMA '29-31 A's
1977 – EPSCC Phila. Favorites #5

Perez-Steele Art postcard

1980 – Perez-Steele HOF #68
1982 – Diamond Classics, #9

1983 – Big League Collectibles, #10

TCMA All-Time Athletics

1983 – TCMA All-Time A's, #5
1988 – World Wide Sports, '33 All-Star
1994 – Megacards, Conlon Collection Cards # 13, 49,

The Duke of Milwaukee

311, 1136,1375 (A's), 1084, 666 (White Sox), 554 (Tigers)
2001 – Upper Deck SP #1

The Duke of Milwaukee

Chapter 12 – The Greatest Team Ever!

Baseball experts have long debated the merits of several teams and have designated one or the other as "The Greatest Team Ever". The one your hear about the most is the 1927 New York Yankees (110-44, 19 games ahead of the second place A's, swept the Pirates in the World Series). An argument has been made for the 1961 Yankees as well (109-53, 8 games ahead of the second place Tigers, beat the Reds 4-to-1 in World Series). And some have added Connie Mack's 1911 A's (101-50, 13.5 games ahead of second place Detroit, beat the Giants 4-to-2 in the World Series).

But in my opinion, and one shared by *Sports Illustrated's* William Nack in 1996, Al Simmons was the horse that pulled Connie Mack's juggernaut wagon in 1929 as they went 104-46, finished a staggering 18 games ahead of Babe Ruth-Lou Gehrig and the Yankees and then took apart a very sound Chicago Cubs team 4 games to one in the World Series. The '29 A's were a blend of young talent, players hitting their prime, and others nearing the end of their careers. It was a combination that worked.

Ticket to the '29 Series, Game 5 – The A's win the title!

Al had a great '29 season, he was 27-years-old and in his prime. He played in 142 games, batted .365 (212 hits, 41 doubles, 34 homers, 157 RBI's).

The Duke of Milwaukee

Who were the rest of these guys?

Playing 141 games at first base was a 21-year-old farm boy from Sudlersville, MD, Jimmie Foxx. Foxx bashed 33 homers, drove in 117 and batted .354. It was his first season as a regular player, though he had made his A's debut in 1925 at age 17. He never played an inning in the minors.

At second base was the marvelous Max Bishop, age 29, who appeared in 129, batted just .232 but was league leader in walks with 128. They called him "camera eye" because he knew the strike zone so well. He fielded .970 for the year.

Joe Boley and Jimmy Dykes split the shortstop position. Boley, 32, played in 88 games and batted .251. Dykes, also 32, played short in 60 games, third base in 45 and second in 12. Dykes batted .327 with 13 homers.

Sammy Hale was on third base more than anyone else. The 32-year-old infielder was in 89 contests at the hot corner hitting .277. His fielding average was .957.

Mickey Cochrane, Jimmy Dykes and Bing Miller, all A's Coaches for the 1950 season – were key members of the '29 club

The Duke of Milwaukee

Sharing the outfield with Simmons were the totally under appreciated Bing Miller, 34, who played in 145 games and batted .335 with 93 RBI's and Mule Haas, 25, who got in to 139 games, batted .313, rapped 16 homers and drove in 82.

The catcher was the immortal Mickey Cochrane, perhaps the finest backstop of all-time. Mickey got in to 135 games, batted .331 with 95 RBI's. He was 26.

On the mound were 29-year-old George "Moose" Earnshaw, who had his best year ever (24-8, 3.28 ERA, 149 k's), Robert "Lefty" Grove, also 29, who won 20, against six losses, a 2.82 ERA and fanned 170 batters. Old reliable Rube Walberg, 32, went 18-11 (3.59 ERA), followed by Eddie Rommel, 31, (12-2, 2.84 ERA), the ageless Jack Quinn (he was actually 45) who crafted an 11-9 mark, Bill Shores, 25 (11-6) and Howard Ehmke, 35, who went 7-2 for the regular season in just 11 appearances and who was the surprise starter in game one of the World Series (winning it 3-1 with a complete game). Other pitchers included Carroll Yerkes (1-0), Bill Breckenridge and Ossie Orwell (0-2).

The '29 A's didn't have much of a bench, mostly because they didn't need it. The veteran Cy Perkins backed up Cochrane at catcher and got in to a total of 38 games (Cloy Mattox backed him in three games), the immortal Eddie Collins, mostly a coach and now 42, was 0-for-7 as a pinch hitter. Backup infielders included George Burns (19 games), Jim Cronin (23 games), Bud Morse, Eric McNair, Rudy Miller, all in less than 10 contests. Spare outfielders included Walt French (10 games), Orwell (who played outfield in 9, pitched in 12), Bevo LeBourveau and 23-year-old Roger "Doc" Cramer who would go on to a long and illustrious big league career after his one game 1929 appearance.

This team boasted four Hall of Famers – Foxx, Simmons, Cochrane and Grove – and two others who should be in the Hall – Miller and Cramer.

Dykes became the second A's manager in history, in 1951. He had been the longtime manager of the Chicago White Sox and, after leaving the A's, managed the Orioles, Reds, Indians and Tigers.

The Duke of Milwaukee

Selected Bibliography

Baseball Anecdotes
Daniel Okrent – Steve Wulf
Harper Perennial Publishers, 1990

My 66 Years in the Big Leagues
Connie Mack
John C. Winston Co., 1950

The Ultimate Phila. A's Reference Book, 1901-54
Ted Taylor
Xlibris Corp., 2010

The Wrecking Crew of '33
Gary A. Sarnoff
McFarland & Co., 2009

Baseball Chronicles
Mike Blake
Betterway Books, 1994

The Baseball Biography Project
Al Simmons by Fred Stein
SABR

Baseball's Forgotten Heroes
Tony Salin
Masters Press, 1999

The Glory of Their Times
Lawrence S. Ritter
Vintage Books 1966, 1984

Now Batting, Number...
Jack Looney
Black Dog & Leventhal Publishers, 2006

Baseball When the Grass Was Real
Donald Honig
Berkeley Medallion Publishing

Baseball Between the Lines
Donald Honig
University of Nebraska Press, 1976

Who's Who In Major League Baseball Yearbooks 1933-1951
Speed Johnson & John P. Carmichael, editors

The Baseball Encyclopedia, 9th Edition
Macmillan Publishing Co., 1993

The Sports Encyclopedia Baseball, 10th edition
D. Neft, R. Cohen, M. Neft
St. Martin's Press, 1999

The Image of their Greatness
Lawrence Ritter and Donald Honig
Crown Publishers, 1979

Baseball-Reference.com
Internet site

The Baseball Biography Project
Al Simmons by Fried Stein
SABR

Bucket foot Al
Dale W. Smith
Phila. A's Historical Society

Baseball Library.com
Internet site

Along the Elephant Trail
Selected Phila. A's Historical Society Newsletters
Ted Taylor, Ernie Montella editors

Also, the Penn State University Library, *SPORT Magazine*, February 1951, *Sports Illustrated* "The Team That Time forgot" by William Nack, August 19, 1996

The Duke of Milwaukee

Epilogue

Since this is my third Philadelphia Athletics-related book in three years people ask me "what's the fascination with a team that left town in 1954. Why don't you channel your energies toward the Phillies?"

Well, the Phillies are a "work in progress" while the A's are clearly defined. They began in 1901, they ended in 1954. They will never lose another game in Philly, they will never break your heart.

Bobby Shantz will always be the '52 MVP, Jimmie Foxx will remain as the "Right-handed Babe Ruth", Al Simmons will always be "Bucket Foot Al" a most unconventional and quite proficient hitter. Lefty Grove will always be the man that other "Lefties" are compared too and no one will ever manage a team (whether they own it or not) as long as the fifty years that Connie Mack did.

My A's books are also a homage to my parents. My father, Jack, who took me to A's games as a small boy; my step-father Ernie Lay, who picked up the responsibility of helping me grow up when his best friend, my father, died leaving an 8-year-old boy…and, of course my mom, Helen, who, while a widow, used to get on the train with me in Glenside, get off at North Broad Street and walk down Lehigh Avenue with me to Shibe Park. Mom may have been the biggest baseball fan of my "three" parents.

Later in life, as founding president of the A's Historical Society I got to meet many of the special men who made the club important to a legion of fans. I never saw Jimmie Foxx play, but he came alive for me because I got to know his daughter, Nanci. I was, at age 15, at Connie Mack's burial in a large Catholic Cemetery in Cheltenham PA Township and felt I got to know Mr. Mack through his daughter Ruth, son Connie Jr., granddaughter Kathy Keim and Senator Connie Mack III.

The A's continue to fascinate me – and other authors – and even though nothing new is happening, there are still things about them waiting to be discovered.

The Duke of Milwaukee

About The Author . . .

Chestnut Hill College Professor *Henry R. (Ted) Taylor*, is a lifelong baseball fan, and was the founding president of The Philadelphia Athletics Historical Society that was formed in 1995 to honor the memory of Philadelphia's American League baseball team. His lectures about the A's and their amazing history over 54 years has been delivered in many venues in the tri-state area.

Ted's most recent book *The Ultimate Philadelphia Athletics Reference Book, 1901-1954 (Xlibris, 2010)* was critically acclaimed and carried by the major book seller Barnes & Noble, by Amazon.com and is on sale at the Phillies ballpark. Critics from as diverse a group as *Baseball Digest, Philadelphia Daily News, Montgomery Media, Mainline Today, Daily Intelligencer, Burlington County NJ Times* and the *Bucks County Courier* all hurled platitudes his way about the book.

Prior to that Taylor had written *The Philadelphia Athletics by the Numbers (2009), 100 years & 100 Recipes, The Story of Ralph's Italian Restaurant (2000), Baseball Cards – 300 All-Time Stars (Publications International)* and *The Official Baseball Card Collecting Handbook (Beekman House)*. Ted has also written two college textbooks on Mass Communications and Public Relations (both published by *Zip Publishing*)..

Widely regarded as an authority on baseball cards and memorabilia, he served as an "expert witness" in the 1979 Federal Anti-Trust suit in U.S. District Court (Fleer vs. Topps). He wrote a "Collectors Corner" column in *The Philadelphia Daily News* for twelve years and was also a columnist for *Sports Collectors Digest*. Ted has had three other baseball-related books published. He often served as host of the nationally syndicated radio show "The Collectibles Hour" on *Sports By-Line USA*, and appeared as a baseball expert on national and local TV. He is owner of TTA Authentic LLC, Abington PA, a sports & celebrity authentication and appraisal company..

The Duke of Milwaukee

A career educator, he has been a teacher, baseball coach, administrator and athletics director. In 1989 his Philadelphia College of Textiles & Science baseball team made it to the NCAA Division II Final 8 and while a college AD his teams won a combined 32 championships in various sports.

Ted served both Fleer and Score Board as a vice president and headed his own public relations firm. He then returned to education, teaching at a Philadelphia area high school for three years and is now an adjunct professor at Chestnut Hill College in Philadelphia since 2000. Taylor served as vice chairman of the board of Act II Playhouse, a professional equity theatre (2000-2010) and is a member of the board of the Celestia Performing Arts Association. He has founded several area youth organizations including the Glenside Youth AC, Keystone State Football League and the Warminster Pioneers and was first president of the Eastern Pennsylvania Sports Collectors Club.

Ted is married, the father of four and grandfather of four, and lives with his wife Cindy in Abington, PA and Wildwood Crest NJ.

INDEX

Note: Al Simmons is mentioned throughout the book and it would be cumbersome – and boring for you the reader – to have to worry about the countless page mentions. It's a book about Al. Similar incidental mentions of the Philadelphia A's (Athletics) baseball club would be excessive, also mentions of the American League. I did, however, list Connie Mack, the man.

A
Aberdeen SD ball club, 3
All-Star game, 30, 32, 33
American Association, 3, 4
Ashburn, Rich, 15
Astroth, Joe, 45

B
Baker, Homerun, 9
Baltimore Orioles, 8, 9, 71
Barrow, Ed, 49
Bender, Chief, 49
Bishop, Max, 17, 19, 20, 70
Blake, Sheriff, 19
Blatz, Ralph, 27
Boley, Joe, 17, 19, 70
Borchert Field, 27
Borchert, Otto, 3
Boston Bees, 38, 39
Boston Red Sox, 10, 12, 40, 44
Boudreau, Lou, 48, 54, 63
Bowes, Mason, 45
Breckenridge, Bill, 71
Bresnahan, Roger, 3
Broeg, Bob, 50
Brooks, Mandy, 27
Brown, Joe E., 13
Brucker, Earle Sr., 46, 52
Burnette, Johnny, 25
Burns, George, 19, 71

The Duke of Milwaukee

Bush, Guy, 17, 18

C
Carmichael, John P., 38
Case, George, 37
Chicago Cubs, 17-20, 69
Chicago White Sox, 23, 25-27, 29, 30, 39, 71
Chichibu, Prince, 25
Christensen, Cuckoo, 27
Cincinnati Reds, 39, 69, 71
Cissell, Bill, 27
Cleveland Indians, 25, 47, 48, 50, 71
Cobb, Ty, 9, 10-12, 23, 50, 54
Cochrane, Mickey, 9, 12, 16, 19, 20, 22, 24, 25, 27, 33, 35, 49, 54, 70, 71
Collins, Eddie Sr., 10, 17, 26, 71
Comiskey Park, 30
Connolly, Tom, 49
Cramer, Roger "Doc", 33, 71
Cronin, Jim, 71
Cronin, Joe, 32, 36, 44, 63
Culberson, Leon, 44
Cunningham, Bruce, 24
Cuyler, KiKi, 17

D
Dakota League, 3
Dean, Dizzy, 49
Detroit Tigers, 35, 36, 39, 69, 71
Dickey, Bill, 12, 32
DiMaggio, Dom, 43, 44
DiMaggio, Vince, 44
Dodge County, Wisconsin, 2
Dunn, Jack, 8, 9
Dykes, Jimmy, 7, 17, 19, 22, 26, 27, 30, 46, 63, 70

E
Earnshaw, George, 17, 18, 22, 23, 30, 71
Eckert, Abbe, 27

Ehmke, Howard, 18, 20, 71

F
Fons, Al, 27
Fonseca, Lou, 30, 63
Fox, Pete, 44
Foxx, Jimmie, 9, 12, 16-19, 21-23, 26, 27, 31-33, 70, 77
Foxx, Nanci (Canaday), 77
French, Larry, 24
French, Walter, 20
Frisch, Frank, 22, 24, 33

G
Galloway, Chick, 7
Gehrig, Lou, 23, 24, 31-34, 69
Gehringer, Charlie, 21, 32
Gelbert, Charley, 22
Gleason, Kid, 10
Gomez, Lefty, 33
Goslin, Goose, 23
Grabiner, Harry, 27
Greaber, Madison, 55
Greaber, Patrick, 2, 33, 51, 55
Griffith, Clark, 21, 36, 37
Griffith, Leon, 45
Grimes, Burleigh, 22
Grove, Lefty, 9, 16-19, 22-25, 32, 49, 71, 77

H
Haas, Mule, 12, 16, 17, 19, 20, 22, 25-27, 71
Hackbarth, Clary, 27
Hafey, Chick, 22
Haines, Jesse, 22
Hale, Sammy, 7, 17, 70
Hall of Fame, 49, 50
Hallahan, Wild Bill, 22, 23, 31
Harder, Mel, 33
Harridge, William, 37
Harris, Bucky, 36, 63

Hauser, Joe, 7, 9
Hebert, Wally, 23
Henderson, Rickey, 51
Heilmann, Harry, 23
Henrich, Tom, 12
Hockenbury, Bill, 45, 46
Honig, Donald, 21, 23, 33, 37
Hoover, Herbert, 20
Hornsby, Rogers, 17, 20, 21
Hubbell, Carl, 32
Hunter, Herb, 24

J
Jackson, Reggie, 51
Jacobson, Baby Doll, 23
Johnson, Ban, 11
Johnson, Harold "Speed", 29
Johnson, Walter, 22
Joost, Eddie, 40
Juneau Millers baseball club, 2

K
Kamm, Willie, 24
Kansas City A's, 53, 54
Keim, Kathy, 77
Kelly, George, 24
Klem, Bill, 49
Knowles, Dr. Leonard, 24
Krausse, Lew, 26
Kubek, Tony Sr., 27

L
Lamar, Bill, 9
Landis, Judge Kenesaw Mountain, 37
Lay, Ernie, 77
Lazzeri, Tony, 32
LeBourveau, Bevo, 71
Lieb, Fred, 24
Lopez, Al, 48, 54

M
Mack, Connie, 2, 3, 7-13, 17, 19, 21, 23, 25, 26, 30, 31, 33, 40, 43, 46, 47, 49, 51, 52, 55, 69, 77
Mack, Connie Jr., 46, 47, 52, 77
Mack, Connie III, 77
Mack, Earle, 46, 47, 52
Mack, Roy, 52, 54
Mack, Ruth (Clark), 77
Malone, Pat, 17-21
Manush, Heine, 32
Maranville, Rabbitt, 24
Mathews, Wid, 4
Mattox, Cloy, 71
McCarthy, Joe, 17, 19, 23, 25
McGowen, Frank, 4
McGraw, John J., 3, 31
McKechnie, Bill, 40, 63
McNair, Eric, 71
Meiji Shrine Stadium, 24
Metkovich, George, 43, 44
Minneapolis Baseball club, 9
Miller, Bing, 16, 17, 19, 20-22, 70, 71
Miller, Rudy, 71
Milwaukee Athletic Club, 49, 55
Milwaukee Brewers, 3
Montella, Ernie, 16
Morse, Bud, 71
Municipal Stadium (Cleveland), 33
Musial, Stan, 41
Myatt, Glenn, 7

N
Nack, William, 16, 69
National League, 22, 37
Naylor, Rollie, 9
Nehf, Art, 19
New York Giants, 3
New York Yankees, 7, 12, 13, 23, 25, 27, 35, 69

The Duke of Milwaukee

O
O'Doul, Lefty, 24
Oliver, Tom, 24
Ormsby, Red, 10, 11
Orwell, Ossie, 71

P
Perkins, Cy, 35, 49, 50, 71
Pipgras, George, 12
Planamente, Joe, 44
Poole, Jim, 9
Portland Baseball club, 9

Q
Quinn, Jack, 18, 71

R
Reader, Doris Lynn, 33
Reardon, John, 24
Rehm, Flint, 22
Robert, Harry, 8
Rommel, Eddie7, 25, 71
Root, Charley, 17-19
Rose, Pete, 15
Rottier, Laura G., 1
Ruel, Muddy. 24
Ruffing, Red, 48
Ruppert, Jacob, 7
Ruth, Babe, 11, 15, 16, 23, 25, 31, 32, 39, 69, 77

S
Saint Adelbert's Cemetery, 55
Salin, Tony, 23
Salt Lake City Baseball club, 8
Scheer, Heine, 4
Schulte, Frank, 15
Sewell, Joe, 23
Shantz, Bobby, 77
Shinners, Ralph, 24

Shibe Park, 7, 18, 20, 23, 77
Shreveport baseball club, 3
Simmons, Al – statistical info, 57-63; collectibles 65-68
Simmons, Alison, 55
Simmons, Daniel, 55
Simmons, David, 55
Simmons, John Alan, 33, 55
Simmons, Karen Ruth (Greaber), 2, 55
Simmons, Wacky, 27
Sisler, George, 23
Speaker, Tris, 10, 12
Sporting News, 15
Sports Illustrated, 16
St. Louis Cardinals. 22, 23
Stengel, Casey, 63
Stevens Point Normal School, 1
Strand, Paul, 7, 8
Street, Gabby, 22
Stephenson, Riggs, 19
Szymanski, Alois/Aloysius (see Al Simmons)

T
Talbot, Gayle, 20
Taylor, Helen, 77
Taylor, Jack, 77
Taylor, Ted, 78-80
Terry, Bill, 32
Texas League, 3
Thomas, Ira, 3
Turner, Tom, 7

W
Walberg, Rube, 17, 19, 20, 22, 71
Waldman, Heide, 55
Walker, Tilly, 7
Ward, Arch, 31
Washington Senators, 8, 10, 21, 22, 36-38, 44
Wheat, Zack, 9
Wilson, Hack, 17, 19

The Duke of Milwaukee

Wilson, Jimmy, 22
Wingo, Red, 7
Wisconsin-Stevens Point, University of, 1
World Series, 17, 21-23, 38, 39, 69
World War I, 7
World War II, 40
Wrigley Field, 20

Y
Yerkes, Carroll, 71
Youmiuri Shimbun, 24

And finally...

I couldn't help but think, once I finished this book, about how different Al Simmons' life would have been had he been born fifty or sixty years later than he was. With his awesome offensive talents, just imagine the salaries that he would have commanded over his long career. It isn't likely he'd have died, alone, on the sidewalk in front of his residence – the Milwaukee Athletic Club – at age 54.

You often hear that Simmons was Gehrig to Foxx's Ruth – the four of them inextricably woven in to the fabric of baseball's "Golden Age".

Ruth grew up in an orphanage in Baltimore, Gehrig in New York City and Simmons in Milwaukee were the sons of immigrant parents and Foxx grew up on a farm in Sudlersville, MD. None of them had it easy from the day they were born. Only Ruth, of the four of them, ever made really big money.

Their lives weren't all that long either. Gehrig died 13 days short of his 38th birthday, Foxx died at 59 and Ruth passed at 53. The money that was there when they played was gone when they didn't. None got to enjoy their old age.

Gehrig died while he still should have been playing, but the rest of them actually did get to retire (though none of them wanted to), and they really didn't enjoy their post playing days very much. Ruth wanted to be a manager – and it was always denied him; Foxx dearly wanted, at least, a big league coaching job after his playing days were over but the very men he made rich with his talents refused him and Simmons, who many expected would one day manage the A's, was fired in the fall-out of a Mack family ownership struggle through no fault of his own, other than, perhaps, he was clearly smarter that Mack's son, Earle, the defacto assistant manager.

They made movies of Ruth ("The Babe Ruth Story" starring William Bendix, perhaps one of the worst baseball movies ever), Gehrig ("Pride of the Yankees" with Gary Cooper, who was a good actor but swung the bat like a girl) and Foxx ("A League of their Own", where Tom Hanks played Jimmy Dugan – clearly supposed to be Foxx, and it was not a flattering, nor accurate, portrayal). Perhaps Simmons was lucky that they

The Duke of Milwaukee

never made a movie about him.

As famous as they were, as adored as they were, they were, in many ways, melancholy figures. Gehrig, reacting to his death sentence from ALS, told a huge gathering at his farewell in Yankee Stadium that he was "the luckiest man on the face of the Earth" (I don't see it, nor do I believe it, brave as it sounded), Ruth, snubbed by baseball after he clearly saved it (following the Black Sox scandal), went to his grave lamenting the missed opportunity he had to manage the Tigers, Foxx managed in the minors and even in the AAGPBL but couldn't get back to the majors, and Simmons' greatest goal, 3000 hits, eluded him by 73.

But in their day they were among the very best, they were fan favorites, they were larger than life and we need to remember that. Like the other three, Al Simmons, perhaps the most overlooked left huge footprints on the landscape of Major League Baseball.

All of these wonderful baseball players should be remembered for what they brought to the ball park and the things they accomplished – I dare say we'll never see their likes again.

- Ted Taylor